Introduction

Precut Quick & Easy Quilts has 10 stunning projects all made with some of the many popular precuts on the market today. Precuts allow you to prepare for your projects in less time and with more accuracy. Each design in this book was selected for its ease of construction, style and consideration for time to stitch it.

The patterns are very versatile and can easily be used for many different purposes. If you're looking for a great lap quilt, there are several, or if you need a great table topper or runner, they're included too. Baby quilts, lap quilts and table accents are all within the pages of this book. All you need to do is to select the right fabric precuts for your goal and you can make these patterns anything you wish. This is designed to be your go-to book for fast and easy patterns you'll choose to make again and again.

Enjoy!

Key for Precut Icons

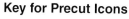

5" Squares	Fat Quarters	10" Squares	2½" Strips

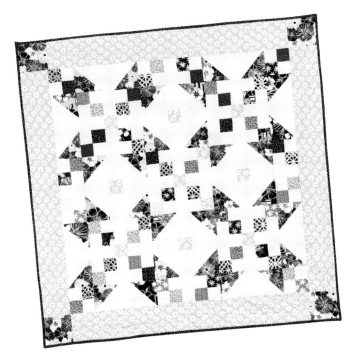

Table of Contents

Bee Party Runner

This table runner is made with only four blocks.
It's a great project for a free afternoon.

Designed & Quilted by Tricia Lynn Maloney

Skill Level
Beginner

Finished Size
Runner Size: 49½" x 15⅜"
Block Size: 8" x 8"
Number of Blocks: 4

Materials
- 12 assorted precut 5" squares; label 4 as D squares
- ⅜ yard dark pink floral print
- ⅜ yard burgundy print
- ⅝ yard yellow tonal
- Backing to size
- Batting to size
- Thread
- Basic sewing tools and supplies

Project Notes
Read all instructions before beginning this project.

Stitch right sides together using a ¼" seam allowance unless otherwise specified.

Materials and cutting lists assume 40" of usable fabric width for yardage.

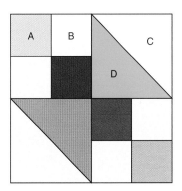

Jacob's Ladder
8" x 8" Finished Block
Make 4

Cutting

From 8 precut squares:
- Cut 16 (2½") A squares.

From dark pink floral print:
- Cut 4 (2½" by fabric width) G/H strips.

From burgundy print:
- Cut 4 (2¼" by fabric width) binding strips.

From yellow tonal:
- Cut 1 (5" by fabric width) strip.
    Subcut strip into 4 (5") C squares and 16 (2½") B squares.
- Cut 1 (12⅝" by fabric width) strip.
    Subcut strip into 2 each 12⅝" E and 6½" F squares. Cut each E square on both diagonals to make 8 triangles. Cut each F square in half on 1 diagonal to make 4 F triangles. Set aside 2 E triangles for another project.

Completing the Blocks

1. Arrange and stitch two A and two B squares into a four-patch unit as shown in Figure 1; press. Repeat to make a total of eight four-patch units.

Four-Patch Unit
Make 8

Figure 1

2. Draw a diagonal line from corner to corner on the wrong side of each C square.

3. Referring to Figure 2, with right sides together, pair a C and D square and stitch ¼" on each side of the drawn line. Cut on the drawn line and press open to make two C-D units. Repeat to make a total of eight C-D units. Trim to 4½" square, keeping seam centered.

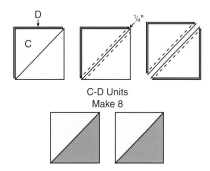

C-D Units
Make 8

Figure 2

4. Arrange two each four-patch and C-D units into rows as shown in Figure 3. Sew units into rows and sew rows together to complete one block; press. Repeat to make a total of four Jacob's Ladder blocks.

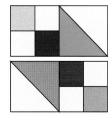

Figure 3

Completing the Runner

1. Referring to Figure 4, arrange and sew an E and F triangle on opposite sides of a block to make an end unit; press. Repeat to make two end units.

End Unit
Make 2

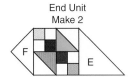

Figure 4

2. Sew an E triangle on opposite sides of a block to make a center unit as shown in Figure 5; press. Repeat to make two center units.

Center Unit
Make 2

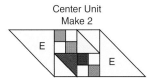

Figure 5

3. Referring to the Assembly Diagram, arrange and stitch center and end units together; add F triangles to remaining corners to complete the runner center; press.

4. Sew G/H strips together on the short ends to make one long strip; press. Subcut strip into two each 2½" x 46" G and 2½" x 15⅞" H strips.

5. Sew G strips to opposite long sides of the runner center and H strips to the short ends to complete the runner top; press.

6. Layer, quilt as desired and bind referring to Quilting Basics on page 47. Sample runner was machine-quilted with an edge-to-edge meander in the center section and a free-motion swirl in the borders. ●

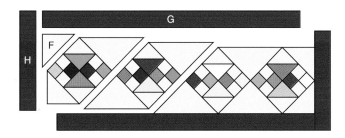

Bee Party Runner
Assembly Diagram 49½" x 15⅜"

Mini Monkey

All you need to make this topper are four fat quarters and a background fabric. Now you can use all those extra fat quarters you've been stashing away for a rainy day and make great table toppers!

Designed & Quilted by Tricia Lynn Maloney

Skill Level
Confident Beginner

Finished Size
Topper Size: 24" x 24"
Block Size: 18" x 18"
Number of Blocks: 1

Materials
- Fat quarter white print
- Fat quarter green print
- Fat quarter pink print
- Fat quarter pink-and-green plaid
- Backing to size
- Batting to size
- Thread
- Basic sewing tools and supplies

Project Notes
Read all instructions before beginning this project.

Stitch right sides together using a ¼" seam allowance unless otherwise specified.

Materials and cutting lists assume 20" of usable fabric width for fat quarters.

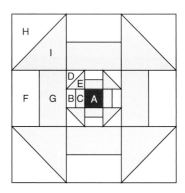

Double Monkey Wrench
18" x 18" Finished Block
Make 1

Cutting

From white print:
- Cut 1 (6½" x 20") strip.
  Subcut strip into 4 (3½" x 6½") F rectangles.
- Cut 1 (6⅞" x 20") strip.
  Subcut strip into 2 (6⅞") H squares.
- Cut 1 (2⅞" x 20") strip.
  Subcut strip into 2 (2⅞") D squares and 4 (1½" x 2½") B rectangles.

From green print:
- Cut 1 (6½" x 20") strip.
  Subcut strip into 4 (3½" x 6½") G rectangles.
- Cut 1 (6⅞" x 20") strip.
  Subcut strip into 2 (6⅞") I squares.
- Cut 1 (2⅞" x 20") strip.
  Subcut strip into 2 (2⅞") E squares and 4 (1½" x 2½") C rectangles.

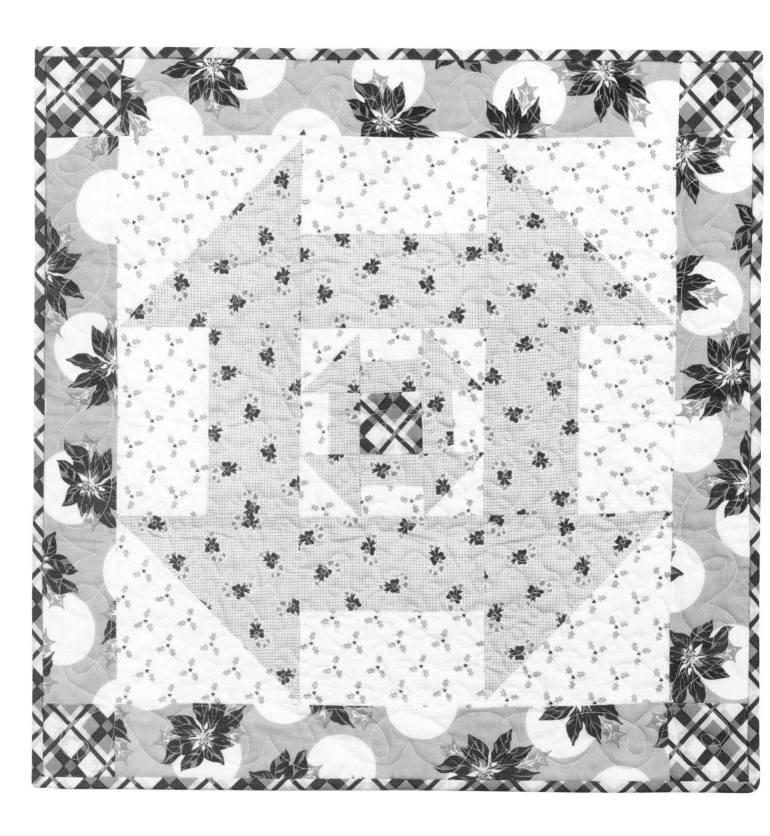

From pink print:
- Cut 4 (3½" x 18½") J strips.

From pink-and-green plaid:
- Cut 5 (2¼" x 20") binding strips.
- Cut 1 (3½" x 20") strip.
  Subcut strip into 4 (3½") K squares and
  1 (2½") A square.

Completing the Blocks

1. Sew a B and C rectangle together to make a B-C unit as shown in Figure 1; press. Repeat to make a total of four B-C units.

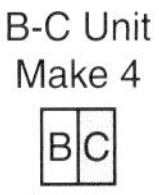

B-C Unit
Make 4

Figure 1

2. Draw a diagonal line from corner to corner on the wrong side of each D and H square.

3. Referring to Figure 2, with right sides together, pair a D and E square and stitch ¼" on both sides of the drawn line. Cut on the drawn line and press open to make two D-E units. Repeat to make a total of four D-E units.

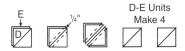

D-E Units
Make 4

Figure 2

4. Arrange and stitch four each D-E and B-C units and one A square into three rows as shown in Figure 3; press. Sew rows together to complete the block center; press.

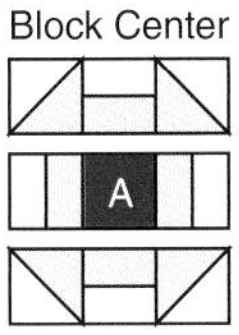

Block Center

Figure 3

5. Referring to Figure 4, sew an F and G rectangle together to make an F-G unit; press. Repeat to make a total of four F-G units.

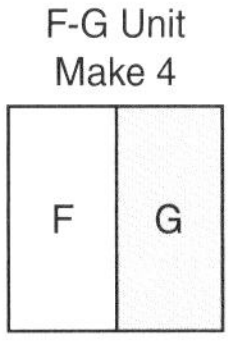

F-G Unit
Make 4

Figure 4

6. Repeat step 3 using H and I squares to make four H-I units as shown in Figure 5.

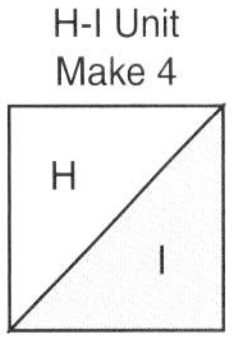

H-I Unit
Make 4

Figure 5

7. Referring to Figure 6, arrange and stitch four each H-I and F-G units and one block center into three rows; press. Sew rows together to complete the Double Monkey Wrench block; press.

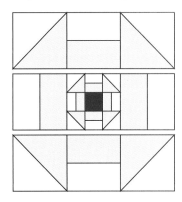

Figure 6

Completing the Topper

1. Referring to the Assembly Diagram, stitch J strips on opposite sides of the block; press.

2. Sew a K square on opposite ends of a J strip to make a J-K strip; press. Repeat to make a second J-K strip.

3. Sew J-K strips to the top and bottom to complete the quilt top; press.

4. Layer, quilt as desired and bind referring to Quilting Basics on page 47. Sample topper was machine-quilted with a free-motion meander in the center section and a loop and arc pattern in the borders. ●

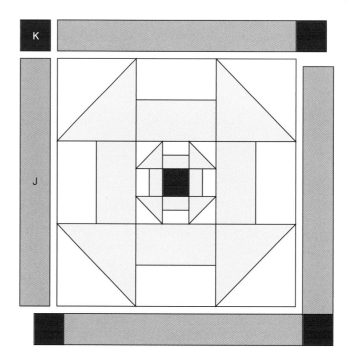

Mini Monkey
Assembly Diagram 24" x 24"

Ziggy Runner

Simple and quick to make, this table runner will be completed before you know it. As an added bonus, you can use any leftover 2½" strips that are just lying around your sewing room.

Designed & Quilted by Gina Gempesaw

Skill Level
Confident Beginner

Finished Size
Runner Size: 46" x 15½"

Materials
- 17 or more assorted bright precut 2½" by fabric width strips
- ⅜ yard blue tonal
- Backing to size
- Batting to size
- Thread
- Basic sewing tools and supplies

Project Notes
Read all instructions before beginning this project.

Stitch right sides together using a ¼" seam allowance unless otherwise specified.

Materials and cutting lists assume 40" of usable fabric width for yardage.

Cutting

From precut strips:
- Cut 81 (2½" x 7½") A rectangles.

From blue tonal:
- Cut 4 (2¼" by fabric width) binding strips.

Completing the Strip Units

A Strip Units
1. With right sides together, position one A rectangle on one end of a second A rectangle as shown in Figure 1. Draw a diagonal line in the direction shown on the wrong side of the top A rectangle. Stitch on the drawn line and trim ¼" away from seam line to make an A-A strip; press.

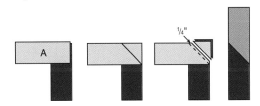

Figure 1

2. Referring to Figure 2, repeat step 1, adding another A rectangle to make an A strip unit. Trim strip unit to measure 2½" x 16", removing the same amount off each end.

A Strip Unit
Make 11

Figure 2

3. Repeat steps 1 and 2 to make a total of 11 A strip units.

B Strip Units

1. With right sides together, position one A rectangle on one end of a second A rectangle as shown in Figure 3. Draw a diagonal line in the direction shown on the wrong side of the top A rectangle. Stitch on the drawn line and trim ¼" away from seam line to make a reverse A-A strip; press.

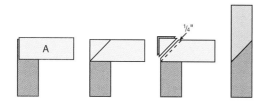

¼"

A

Figure 3

2. Referring to Figure 4, repeat step 2 of A Strip Units, adding two more A rectangles to make a B strip unit. Trim strip unit to measure 2½" x 16", removing the same amount off each end.

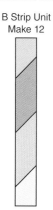

B Strip Unit
Make 12

Figure 4

3. Repeat steps 1 and 2 to make a total of 12 B strip units.

Completing the Runner

1. Referring to the Assembly Diagram, arrange and stitch A and B strip units alternately together to complete the runner top; press.

2. Layer, quilt as desired and bind referring to Quilting Basics on page 47. Sample runner was machine-quilted with wavy-line quilting. ●

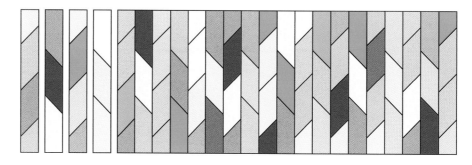

Ziggy Runner
Assembly Diagram 46" x 15½"

Indian Summer Topper

This is the perfect project to use leftover precut 5" squares that keep building up around your sewing room. All you need to select is a good background fabric and one more accent fabric.

Designed & Quilted by Carolyn S. Vagts

Skill Level
Confident Beginner

Finished Size
Topper Size: 28" x 28"
Block Size: 12" x 12"
Number of Blocks: 4

Materials
- 10 or more assorted precut 5" batik squares
- ⅝ yard brown batik
- ¾ yard cream batik
- Backing to size
- Batting to size
- Thread
- Basic sewing tools and supplies

Project Notes
Read all instructions before beginning this project.

Stitch right sides together using a ¼" seam allowance unless otherwise specified.

Materials and cutting lists assume 40" of usable fabric width for yardage.

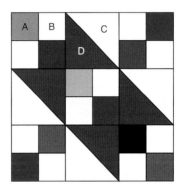

Jacob's Ladder
12" x 12" Finished Block
Make 4

Cutting

From precut 5" squares:
- Cut 40 (2½") A squares.

From brown batik:
- Cut 1 (4⅞" by fabric width) strip.
  Subcut strip into 8 (4⅞") D squares.
- Cut 4 (2¼" by fabric width) binding strips.

From cream batik:
- Cut 3 (2½" by fabric width) strips.
  Subcut strips into 40 (2½") B squares.
- Cut 1 (4⅞" by fabric width) strip.
  Subcut strip into 8 (4⅞") C squares.
- Cut 4 (2½" by fabric width) strips.
  Subcut strips into 2 each 2½" x 24½" E
  and 2½" x 28½" F strips.

Completing the Blocks

1. Arrange and sew two each A and B squares into two rows as shown in Figure 1; press. Sew rows together to make a four-patch unit; press. Repeat to make a total of 20 four-patch units.

Four-Patch Unit
Make 20

Figure 1

2. Draw a diagonal line from corner to corner on the wrong side of each C square.

3. Referring to Figure 2, with right sides together, pair a C and D square and stitch ¼" on both sides of the drawn line. Cut on the drawn line and press open to make two C-D units. Repeat to make a total of 16 C-D units.

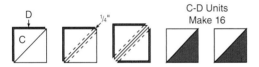

Figure 2

4. Arrange and stitch four C-D units and five four-patch units into three rows as shown in Figure 3; press. Sew rows together to complete one Jacob's Ladder block; press. Repeat to make a total of four blocks.

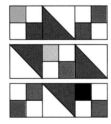

Figure 3

Completing the Topper

1. Referring to the Assembly Diagram, join two blocks to make a row; press. Repeat to make a second row.

2. Join the rows to complete the topper center; press.

3. Stitch E strips to opposite sides and F strips to the top and bottom of the topper center to complete the top; press.

4. Layer, quilt as desired and bind referring to Quilting Basics on page 47. Sample topper was machine-quilted with a free-motion meander in the background sections. ●

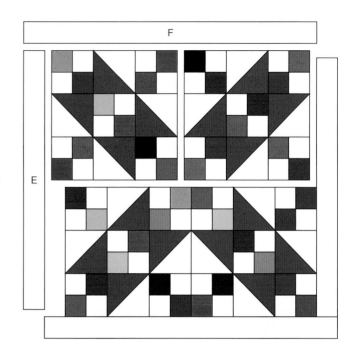

Indian Summer Topper
Assembly Diagram 28" x 28"

Crossroads

Make this striking quilt with just 18 precut
2½" strips and a background fabric!

Design by Lyn Brown
Quilted by Rebecca Sproal

Skill Level
Confident Beginner

Finished Size
Quilt Size: 58" x 80"
Block Size: 18" x 18"
Number of Blocks: 6

Materials
- 18 assorted precut 2½" by fabric width strips; sort into 6 color groups of 3 strips each
- ⅔ yard cream-with-black print
- 3¾ yards white solid
- Backing to size
- Batting to size
- Thread
- Basic sewing tools and supplies

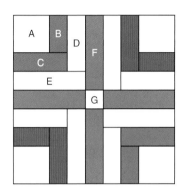

Crossroads
18" x 18" Finished Block
Make 6

Project Notes
Read all instructions before beginning this project.

Stitch right sides together using a ¼" seam allowance unless otherwise specified.

Materials and cutting lists assume 41" of usable fabric width for yardage.

Cutting

From each color group of 3 precut strips:

- Cut 2 each 2½" x 4½" B rectangles and 2½" x 6½" C strips from 1 strip; repeat with second strip to total 4 each B and C.
- Cut 4 (2½" x 8½") F strips from the third strip.

From cream-with-black print:

- Cut 8 (2¼" by fabric width) binding strips.

From white solid:

- Cut 7 (4½" by fabric width) strips.
    Subcut strips into 2 (4½" x 40½") I strips,
        3 (4½" x 18½") H strips and 24 (4½") A squares.
- Cut 2 (6½" by fabric width) strips.
    Subcut strips into 24 (2½" x 6½") D strips.
- Cut 2 (8½" by fabric width) strips.
    Subcut strips into 24 (2½" x 8½") E strips and
        6 (2½") G squares.
- Cut 1 (62½" by fabric width) strip.
    Subcut strip lengthwise into 2 each 9½" x 62½" J
        and 9½" x 58½" K strips.

Completing the Blocks

1. To make one block, select one color group of B, C and F strips; four each A squares and D and E strips; and one G square.

2. Sew an A square and B rectangle together to make an A-B unit as shown in Figure 1; press. Repeat to make a total of four A-B units.

A-B Unit
Make 4

Figure 1

3. Referring to Figure 2, sew a matching C strip to one long side of the A-B unit to make an A-B-C unit; press. Repeat to make a total of four A-B-C units.

A-B-C Unit
Make 4

Figure 2

4. Arrange and sew a D and E strip to the B and C sides of an A-B-C unit as shown in Figure 3 to make a quarter-block unit; press. Repeat to make a total of four quarter-block units.

Quarter-Block Unit
Make 4

Figure 3

5. Referring to Figure 4, sew a G square between two F strips to make an F-G unit; press.

F-G Unit
Make 1

Figure 4

6. Arrange four quarter-block units, two F strips and the F-G unit as shown in Figure 5. Sew quarter-block units and F strips into two rows; press. Sew rows on opposite sides of the F-G unit to complete one block.

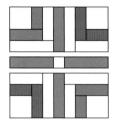

Figure 5

7. Repeat steps 1–6 to make a total of six Crossroads blocks.

Completing the Quilt

1. Referring to Figure 6, arrange and sew two blocks on opposite sides of an H strip to make a block row; press. Repeat to make a total of three block rows.

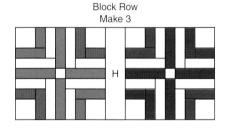

Block Row
Make 3

Figure 6

2. Referring to the Assembly Diagram, alternately arrange and stitch block rows and I strips together to complete the quilt center; press.

3. Sew J strips to opposite sides of the quilt center and K strips to the top and bottom to complete the quilt top; press.

4. Layer, quilt as desired and bind referring to Quilting Basics on page 47. Sample quilt was machine-quilted with an edge-to-edge modern geometric pattern. ●

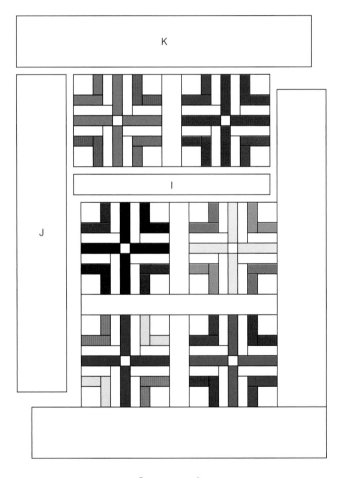

Crossroads
Assembly Diagram 58" x 80"

Hop, Skip, Jump

You can make two quilts from a pack of 40 precut 10" squares using this pattern. The block is super easy to make, and the quilt can be sewn together really fast. It's a great pattern for beginners who want to practice matching seams.

Design by Gina Gempesaw
Quilted by Anne Cowan

Skill Level
Confident Beginner

Finished Size
Quilt Size: 44" x 54"
Block Size: 10" x 10"
Number of Blocks: 20

Materials
- 20 assorted precut 10" squares
- ⅝ yard green tonal
- ⅝ yard light gray tonal
- ¾ yard white solid
- Backing to size
- Batting to size
- Thread
- Basic sewing tools and supplies

Project Notes
Read all instructions before beginning this project.

Stitch right sides together using a ¼" seam allowance unless otherwise specified.

Materials and cutting lists assume 40" of usable fabric width for yardage.

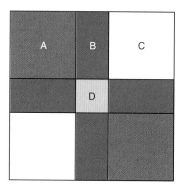

Hop, Skip, Jump
10" x 10" Finished Block
Make 20

Cutting

From each precut square:
- Referring to Figure 1, cut 2 (4½") A squares and 4 (2½" x 4½") B rectangles for a total of 40 A squares and 80 B rectangles.

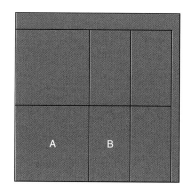

Figure 1

From green tonal:
- Cut 6 (2¼" by fabric width) binding strips.

From light gray tonal:
- Cut 2 (2½" by fabric width) strips.
  Subcut strips into 20 (2½") D squares.
- Cut 5 (2½" by fabric width) E/F strips.

From white solid:
- Cut 5 (4½" by fabric width) strips.
  Subcut strips into 40 (4½") C squares.

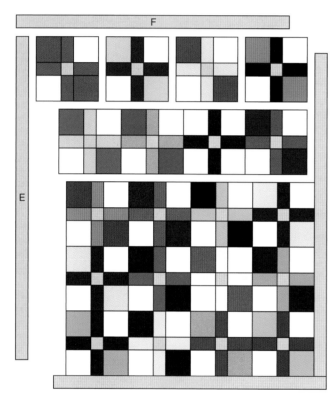

Hop, Skip, Jump
Assembly Diagram 44" x 54"

Completing the Blocks

1. To complete one block, select four same-fabric B rectangles, two each same-fabric A and C squares, and one D square.

2. Referring to Figure 2, arrange A, B, C and D pieces into three rows. Sew pieces into rows and sew rows together to complete one block; press. Repeat to make a total of 20 blocks.

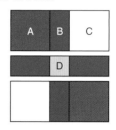

Figure 2

Completing the Quilt

1. Referring to the Assembly Diagram, arrange blocks into five rows of four blocks each. Sew into rows; press. Sew the rows together to complete the quilt center; press.

2. Sew E/F strips together on the short ends to make one long strip; press. Subcut strip into two each 2½" x 50½" E and 2½" x 44½" F strips.

3. Sew E strips to opposite sides of the quilt center and F strips to the top and bottom to complete the quilt top; press.

4. Layer, quilt as desired and bind referring to Quilting Basics on page 47. Sample quilt was machine-quilted with an edge-to-edge swirl design. ●

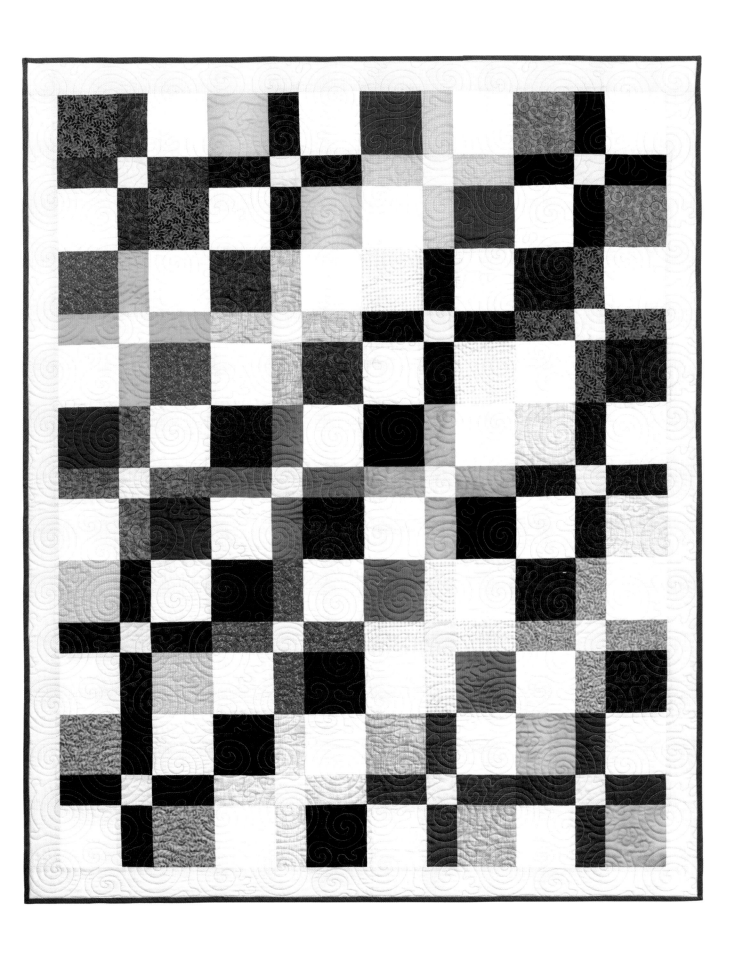

Baby Stars

As another option for this pattern, try fussy-cutting novelty prints for the center squares to achieve a personalized finish.

Designed & Quilted by Bev Getschel

Skill Level

Intermediate

Finished Size

Quilt Size: 43" x 43"
Block Size: 13" x 13"
Number of Blocks: 9

Materials

- 18 assorted precut 2½" by fabric width strips
- Fat quarter each gray and apricot batiks
- ⅝ yard aqua batik
- ⅞ yard dark blue batik
- Backing to size
- Batting to size
- Thread
- Basic sewing tools and supplies

Project Notes

Read all instructions before beginning this project.

Stitch right sides together using a ¼" seam allowance unless otherwise specified.

Materials and cutting lists assume 40" of usable fabric width for yardage.

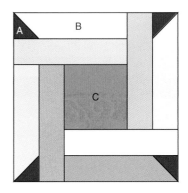

Baby Stars
13" x 13" Finished Block
Make 9

Cutting

From each precut strip:

Cut 4 (2½" x 9½") B strips for a total of 72 B strips.

From gray batik:

- Cut 4 (5½") C squares.

From apricot batik:

- Cut 4 (5½") C squares.

From aqua batik:

- Cut 1 (11½" by fabric width) strip.
  Subcut strip into 12 (2½" x 11½") D strips and 1 (5½") C square.
- Cut 1 (2⅞" by fabric width) strip.
  Subcut strip into 8 (2⅞") E squares.

From dark blue batik:

- Cut 3 (2½" by fabric width) strips.
  Subcut strips into 48 (2½") A squares.
- Cut 1 (2⅞" by fabric width) strip.
  Subcut strip into 8 (2⅞") F squares.
- Cut 5 (2¼" by fabric width) binding strips.

Completing the Blocks

1. Draw a diagonal line from corner to corner on the wrong side of the A and F squares.

2. Position an A square on one end of a B strip, right sides together, and stitch on the drawn line as shown in Figure 1. Trim ¼" past seam line and press open to make an A-B unit. Repeat to make a total of 36 A-B units.

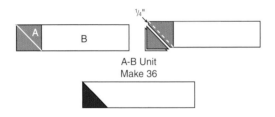

A-B Unit
Make 36

Figure 1

3. Referring to Figure 2, arrange and stitch an A-B unit and B strip together on one long side to make an A-B-B unit; press. Repeat to make a total of 36 A-B-B units.

A-B-B Unit
Make 36

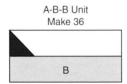

Figure 2

4. Referring to Sewing Partial Seams on page 34 and the block drawing, arrange and stitch four A-B-B units to a C square to complete one Baby Stars block; press. Repeat to make a total of nine blocks.

5. Referring to Figure 3, position an A square on one end of a D strip, right sides together, and stitch on the drawn line. Trim ¼" past seam line and press open to make an A-D unit. Repeat to make a total of 12 A-D units.

A-D Unit
Make 12

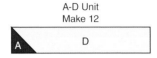

Figure 3

6. Referring to Figure 4, pair an E and F square, right sides together, and stitch ¼" on both sides of the drawn line. Cut on the drawn line; press open to make two E-F units. Repeat to make a total of 16 E-F units.

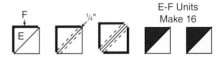

Figure 4

Completing the Quilt

1. Referring to the Assembly Diagram, arrange the blocks into three rows of three blocks each. Sew blocks into rows and sew the rows together to complete the quilt center; press.

2. Arrange and sew three A-D units alternately together with three E-F units to make a side border as shown in Figure 5; press. Repeat to make a second side border.

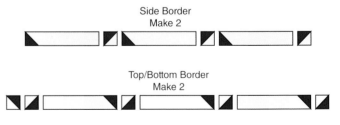

Side Border
Make 2

Top/Bottom Border
Make 2

Figure 5

3. Again referring to Figure 5, arrange and sew three A-D units alternately together with four E-F units; add an additional E-F unit to one end of border strip as shown to make a top/bottom border; press. Repeat to make a second top/bottom border.

4. Arrange and stitch side borders to opposite sides of the quilt center and top/bottom borders to the top and bottom to complete the quilt top; press.

5. Layer, quilt as desired and bind referring to Quilting Basics on page 47. Sample quilt was custom-quilted with a heart motif in each C square, echoed lines around each pinwheel and a free-motion background meander. ●

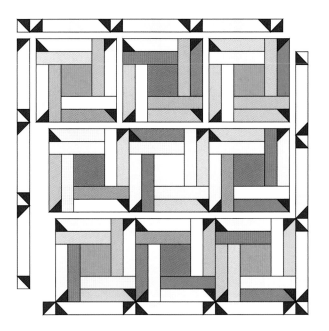

Baby Stars
Assembly Diagram 43" x 43"

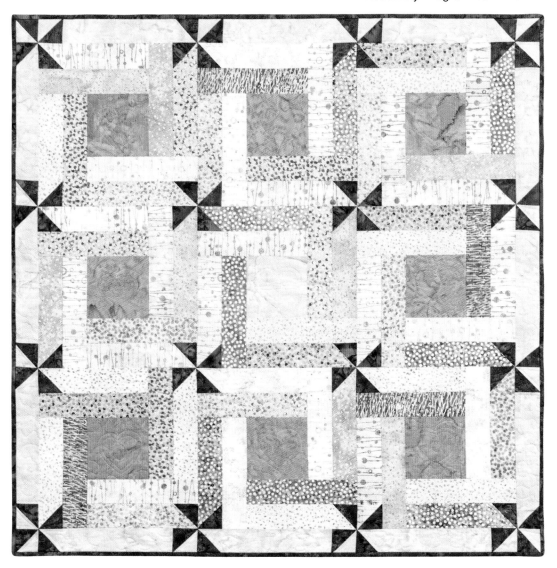

Sewing Partial Seams

Partial Seams

Use partial seaming to join a variety of unevenly placed pieces in a block or unevenly placed blocks or sections in a quilt.

1. Lay out the block pieces or quilt sections around the center piece or block as shown in Figure A.

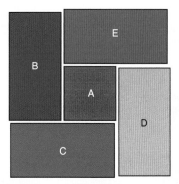

Figure A

2. Referring to Figure B, stitch A (center square) to B (first section) beginning approximately 2" from the bottom corner of A. Finger-press A away from B.

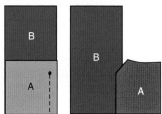

Figure B

3. Working counterclockwise, join C (second section) to the A-B unit as shown in Figure C, stitching the entire length of the seam. Press seam toward C.

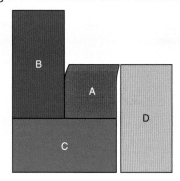

Figure C

4. Match and join D (third section) to A-C edge referring again to Figure C, completing the entire length of the seam. Press seam toward D.

5. Join E (fourth section) to the A-D edge, again completing the entire length of the seam, as shown in Figure D. Be sure to keep B (first section) out of the way when stitching.

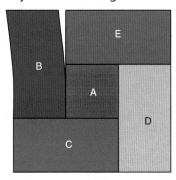

Figure D

6. Complete the assembly by finishing the A-B seam that was partially sewn in step 2. Fold over C and match the B edge to the A-E edge. Lower the machine needle at the end of the A-B seam, backstitch to secure and complete the A-B seam as shown in red in Figure E. Press seam toward B, completing the block or quilt section (Figure F).

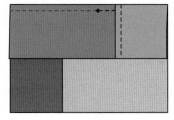

Figure E

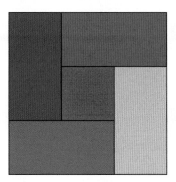

Figure F

Braid My Way!

This quilt is a great way to use 10" precut squares in a unique way. Don't worry about the color placement. It all works out in the end.

Design by Karen DuMont of KariePatch Designs
Quilted by Sara Parrish

Skill Level
Intermediate

Finished Size
Quilt Size: 66" x 66"
Block Size: 9" x 9"
Number of Blocks: 36

Materials
- 42 assorted bright precut 10" squares
- 20 assorted dark precut 10" squares
- ½ yard yellow tonal
- ⅝ yard dark blue tonal
- 1⅛ yards dark blue print
- Backing to size
- Batting to size
- Thread
- Basic sewing tools and supplies

Project Notes
Read all instructions before beginning this project.

Stitch right sides together using a ¼" seam allowance unless otherwise specified.

Materials and cutting lists assume 40" of usable fabric width for yardage.

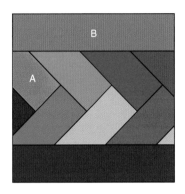

Braid
9" x 9" Finished Block
Make 36

Cutting

From bright precut 10" squares:
- Cut 324 (2½" x 5") A rectangles.

From dark precut 10" squares:
- Cut 72 (2½" x 9½") B rectangles.

From yellow tonal:
- Cut 6 (2" by fabric width) C/D strips.

From dark blue tonal:
- Cut 7 (2¼" by fabric width) binding strips.

From dark blue print:
- Cut 7 (5" by fabric width) E/F strips.

Completing the Blocks

1. To make one block, select nine different A rectangles.

2. Sew the short side of one A rectangle to the long side of a second A rectangle as shown in Figure 1; press.

Figure 1

3. Referring to Figure 2, sew a third A rectangle to the left side of the braid; press.

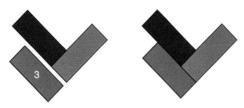

Figure 2

4. Sew a fourth A rectangle to the right side of the braid as shown in Figure 3; press.

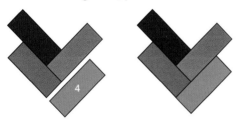

Figure 3

5. Referring to Figure 4, continue adding A rectangles to opposite sides of the braid until all nine A rectangles have been stitched in place; press.

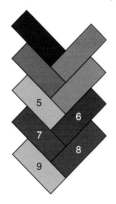

Figure 4

6. Trim the braid to 5½" x 9½," using a cutting grid and rotary cutter. Align the cutting grid along the inner points on both sides of the braid as shown in Figure 5 to complete one braid unit.

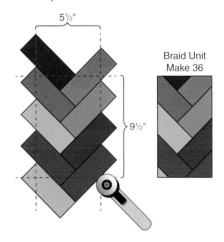

Figure 5

7. Referring to the block drawing, sew B strips to opposite long sides of the braid unit to complete one Braid block; press.

8. Repeat steps 1–7 to make a total of 36 Braid blocks.

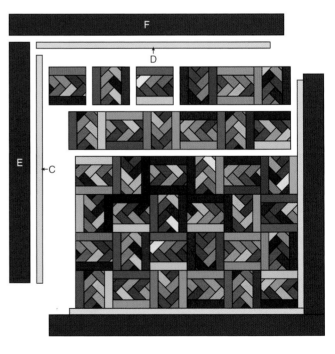

Braid My Way!
Assembly Diagram 66" x 66"

Completing the Quilt

1. Referring to the Assembly Diagram, arrange the blocks into six rows of six blocks each, turning every other block in each row. Sew blocks into rows and sew the rows together to complete the quilt center; press.

2. Sew C/D strips together on the short ends to make one long strip; press. Subcut strip into two each 2" x 54½" C and 2" x 57½" D strips.

3. Sew C strips to opposite sides of the quilt center and D strips to the top and bottom; press.

4. Sew E/F strips together on the short ends to make one long strip; press. Subcut strip into two each 2" x 57½" E and 2" x 66½" F strips.

5. Sew E strips to opposite sides of the quilt center and F strips to the top and bottom to complete the quilt top; press.

6. Layer, quilt as desired and bind referring to Quilting Basics on page 47. Sample quilt was machine-quilted with an edge-to-edge feather swirl pattern. ●

Lemon Drop

Divide precut 5" squares into four 2½" squares to create these blocks. Twist and turn the blocks to see different ways you might set them into a quilt. Discover several quilt possibilities!

Designed & Quilted by Tricia Lynn Maloney

Skill Level
Beginner

Finished Size
Quilt Size: 47" x 47"
Block Size: 8" x 8"
Number of Blocks: 16

Materials
- 16 assorted precut 5" squares
- 20 black floral print precut 5" D squares or ⅝ yard black floral print
- ½ yard black dot
- ⅞ yard yellow floral print
- 1⅓ yards white solid
- Backing to size
- Batting to size
- Thread
- Basic sewing tools and supplies

Project Notes
Read all instructions before beginning this project.

Stitch right sides together using a ¼" seam allowance unless otherwise specified.

Materials and cutting lists assume 40" of usable fabric width for yardage.

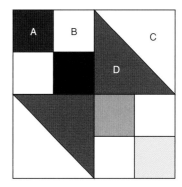

Jacob's Ladder
8" x 8" Finished Block
Make 16

Cutting

From 16 assorted precut 5" squares:
- Cut 64 (2½") A squares.

From black floral print (if not using precut squares):
- Cut 3 (5" by fabric width) strips.
  Subcut strips into 20 (5") D squares.

From black dot:
- Cut 5 (2¼" by fabric width) binding strips.

From yellow floral print:
- Cut 1 (2½" by fabric width) strip.
  Subcut strip into 9 (2½") F squares.
- Cut 4 (5" by fabric width) strips.
  Subcut strips into 4 (5" x 38½") G strips.

From white solid:
- Cut 11 (2½" by fabric width) strips.
  Subcut strips into 24 (2½" x 8½") E rectangles
  and 64 (2½") B squares.
- Cut 2 (5" by fabric width) strips.
  Subcut strips into 16 (5") C squares.

Completing the Blocks

1. Arrange and stitch two A and two B squares into a four-patch unit as shown in Figure 1; press. Repeat to make a total of 32 four-patch units.

Four-Patch Unit
Make 32

Figure 1

2. Draw a diagonal line from corner to corner on the wrong side of each C square.

3. Referring to Figure 2, with right sides together, pair a C and D square and stitch ¼" on each side of the drawn line. Cut on the drawn line and press open to make two C-D units. Repeat to make a total of 32 C-D units. Trim to 4½" square, keeping the seam centered.

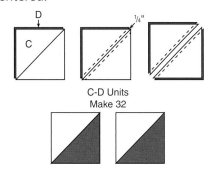

C-D Units
Make 32

Figure 2

4. Arrange two each four-patch and C-D units into rows as shown in Figure 3. Sew units into rows and sew rows together to complete one Jacob's Ladder block; press. Repeat to make a total of 16 blocks.

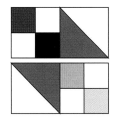

Figure 3

Completing the Quilt

1. Referring to Figure 4, arrange and sew four blocks alternately together with three E strips to make a block row; press. Repeat to make a total of four block rows.

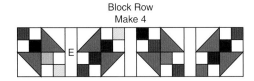

Block Row
Make 4

Figure 4

2. Sew four E rectangles alternately together with three F squares to make a sashing row as shown in Figure 5; press. Repeat to make a total of three sashing rows.

Sashing Row
Make 3

Figure 5

3. Referring to the Assembly Diagram, arrange and join block rows and sashing rows to complete the quilt center; press.

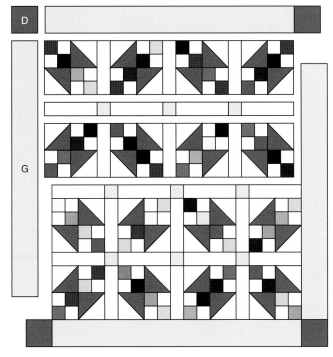

Lemon Drop
Assembly Diagram 47" x 47"

4. Sew a D square on opposite ends of a G strip to make a D-G strip; press. Repeat to make a second D-G strip.

5. Sew G strips to opposite sides of the quilt center and D-G strips to the top and bottom to complete the quilt top; press.

6. Layer, quilt as desired and bind referring to Quilting Basics on page 47. Sample quilt was machine-quilted with a floral meander in the center section and a free-motion arcs in the borders. ●

Charmingly Scrappy

This pattern has the option to use either 5" or 10" precut squares. Pick coordinating fabrics to accompany your selected precuts and start stitching!

Design by Nancy Scott
Quilted by Masterpiece Quilting

Skill Level
Confident Beginner

Finished Size
Quilt Size: 59" x 68½"
Block Size: 7½" x 7½"
Number of Blocks: 36

Materials
- 35 precut 10" squares or 100 precut 5" squares assorted batiks
- ⅝ yard light green batik
- 1⅔ yards light purple batik
- 1⅞ yards dark purple batik
- Backing to size
- Batting to size
- Fusible web with paper release
- Template material
- Thread
- Basic sewing tools and supplies

Project Notes
Read all instructions before beginning this project.

Stitch right sides together using a ¼" seam allowance unless otherwise specified.

Materials and cutting lists assume 40" of usable fabric width for yardage.

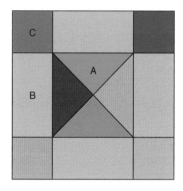

Charmingly Scrappy
7½" x 7½" Finished Block
Make 36

Cutting

From each of 18 precut 10" squares or from precut 5" squares:
- Cut 2 (5") A squares from each 10" square for a total of 36 A squares. Alternately, select 36 precut 5" squares for A.

From remainder of 5" or 10" precut squares:
- From each of 14 (10") squares, cut 1 (5") square or select 14 (5") squares; set aside for flower appliqués.
- Cut 200 (2½") C squares from remainder of squares.

From light green batik:
- Cut 7 (2¼" by fabric width) binding strips.

From light purple batik:
- Cut 2 (8" by fabric width) strips.
  Subcut strips into 6 (8") E squares and 16 (2½" x 4") B rectangles.
- Cut 8 (4" by fabric width) strips.
  Subcut strips into 128 (2½" x 4") B strips to total 144 B rectangles.

From dark purple batik:
- Cut 7 (8" by fabric width) strips.
  Subcut strips into 97 (2½" x 8") D strips.

Completing the Blocks

1. Draw a diagonal line from corner to corner on the wrong side of 18 A squares.

2. Pair a marked and unmarked A square with right sides together and stitch ¼" on both sides of drawn line as shown in Figure 1. Cut on drawn line and press open to make two A-A units. Repeat to make a total of 36 A-A units.

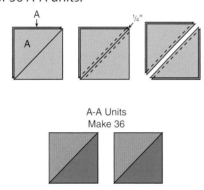

A-A Units
Make 36

Figure 1

3. Draw a diagonal line from corner to corner on the wrong side of 18 A-A units, perpendicular to the seam.

4. Referring to Figure 2, pair a marked and unmarked A-A unit with right sides together, matching seams. Stitch ¼" on both sides of drawn line. Cut on drawn line and press open to make two hourglass units. Repeat to make a total of 36 hourglass units. Trim units to measure 4" square, keeping diagonal seams centered.

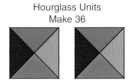

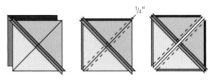

Hourglass Units
Make 36

Figure 2

5. Sew a B rectangle to opposite sides of an hourglass unit to make a block center row as shown in Figure 3; press. Repeat to make a total of 36 block center rows.

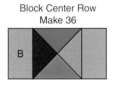

Block Center Row
Make 36

Figure 3

6. Referring to Figure 4, sew a C square to opposite ends of a B rectangle to make a B-C strip; press. Repeat to make a total of 72 B-C strips.

B-C Strip
Make 72

Figure 4

7. Sew a B-C strip to the top and bottom of a block center row to complete one Charmingly Scrappy block as shown in Figure 5; press. Repeat to make a total of 36 blocks.

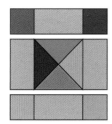

Figure 5

Completing the Quilt

Refer to the Assembly Diagram for construction steps and project photo for appliqué placement.

1. Referring to Figure 6, alternately sew seven C squares and six D strips together to make a sashing row. Repeat to make a total of eight sashing rows.

Sashing Row
Make 8

Figure 6

2. Sew seven D strips, two E squares and four pieced blocks to make a row; press. Repeat to make two rows.

3. Sew seven D strips, one E square and five pieced blocks to make a row; press. Repeat to make two rows.

4. Sew seven D strips and six pieced blocks to make a row; press. Repeat to make a total of three rows.

5. Arrange and sew block rows and sashing rows together to complete the quilt top center; press.

Adding the Appliqués

1. Prepare flower template using provided pattern.

2. Trace 14 flower shapes on the paper side of the fusible web.

3. Cut out with a narrow margin.

4. Fuse on the wrong side of 5" squares set aside for flowers.

5. Cut out on drawn line and remove paper backing.

6. Referring to the project photo, position the flower appliqués on the E squares and sashing in opposite corners. When satisfied with the arrangement, fuse in place.

7. Machine-stitch to secure edges to complete the quilt top. On the sample quilt the appliqués were stitched with a reduced straight stitch.

8. Layer, quilt as desired and bind referring to Quilting Basics on page 47. Sample quilt was machine-quilted with an edge-to-edge floral pattern. ●

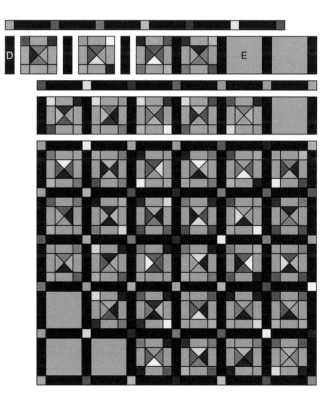

Charmingly Scrappy
Assembly Diagram 59" x 68½"

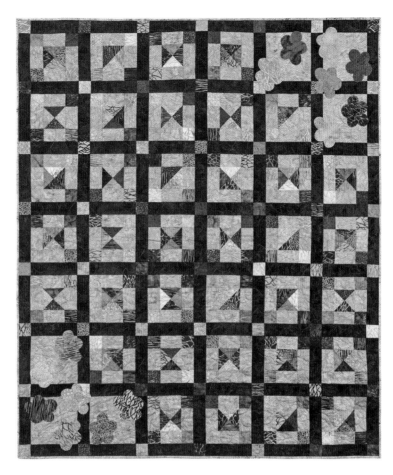

Charmingly Scrappy
Flower
Cut as per instructions

Quilting Basics

The following is a reference guide. For more information, consult a comprehensive quilting book.

Quilt Backing & Batting

We suggest that you cut your backing and batting 8" larger than the finished quilt-top size. If preparing the backing from standard-width fabrics, remove the selvages and sew two or three lengths together; press seams open. If using 108"-wide fabric, trim to size on the straight grain of the fabric.

Prepare batting the same size as your backing. You can purchase prepackaged sizes or battings by the yard and trim to size.

Quilting

1. Press quilt top on both sides and trim all loose threads.

2. Make a quilt sandwich by layering the backing right side down, batting and quilt top centered right side up on flat surface and smooth out. Pin or baste layers together to hold.

3. Mark quilting design on quilt top and quilt as desired by hand or machine. **Note:** *If you are sending your quilt to a professional quilter, contact them for specifics about preparing your quilt for quilting.*

4. When quilting is complete, remove pins or basting. Trim batting and backing edges even with raw edges of quilt top.

Binding the Quilt

1. Join binding strips on short ends with diagonal seams to make one long strip; trim seams to ¼" and press seams open (Figure A).

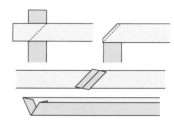

Figure A

2. Fold 1" of one short end to wrong side and press. Fold the binding strip in half with wrong sides together along length, again referring to Figure A; press.

3. Starting about 3" from the folded short end, sew binding to quilt top edges, matching raw edges and using a ¼" seam. Stop stitching ¼" from corner and backstitch (Figure B).

Stop ¼"

Figure B

4. Fold binding up at a 45-degree angle to seam and then down even with quilt edges, forming a pleat at corner, referring to Figure C.

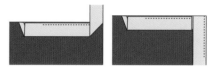

Figure C

5. Resume stitching from corner edge as shown in Figure C, down quilt side, backstitching ¼" from next corner. Repeat, mitering all corners, stitching to within 3" of starting point.

6. Trim binding end long enough to tuck inside starting end and complete stitching (Figure D).

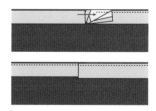

Figure D

7. Fold binding to quilt back and stitch in place by hand or machine to complete your quilt.

Special Thanks

Please join us in thanking the talented designers
whose work is featured in this collection.

Lyn Brown
Crossroads, page 21

Karen DuMont of KariePatch Designs
Braid My Way!, page 35

Gina Gempesaw
Hop, Skip, Jump, page 26
Ziggy Runner, page 13

Bev Getschel
Baby Stars, page 30

Tricia Lynn Maloney
Bee Party Runner, page 3
Lemon Drop, page 39
Mini Monkey, page 8

Nancy Scott
Charmingly Scrappy, page 43

Carolyn S. Vagts
Indian Summer Topper, page 17

Supplies

We would like to thank the following manufacturers who provided
materials to our designers to make sample projects for this book.

Bee Party Runner, page 3: Front Porch collection from Benartex

Indian Summer Topper, page 17: Tuscany Cotton Wool batting from Hobbs

Crossroads, page 21: Bali Poppy batiks from Hoffman California-International Fabrics

Baby Stars, page 30: Bali Poppy and 1895 series batiks from Hoffman California-International Fabrics and Nature-Fil bamboo-blend batting from Fairfield

Lemon Drop, page 39: Lemon Twist collection from Benartex

Charmingly Scrappy, page 43: City Culture 2 collection and yardage from Island Batik, and Lite Steam-A-Seam 2 and Warm 80/20 batting from The Warm Company

 Published by Annie's, 306 East Parr Road, Berne, IN 46711. Printed in USA. Copyright © 2018, 2021 Annie's. All rights reserved. This publication may not be reproduced in part or in whole without written permission from the publisher.

RETAIL STORES: If you would like to carry this publication or any other Annie's publications, visit AnniesWSL.com.

Every effort has been made to ensure that the instructions in this publication are complete and accurate. We cannot, however, take responsibility for human error, typographical mistakes or variations in individual work. Please visit AnniesCustomerService.com to check for pattern updates.

ISBN: 978-1-64025-046-8

6 7 8 9